A
TIME THERE
WAS

a story of rock art, bees and Bushmen

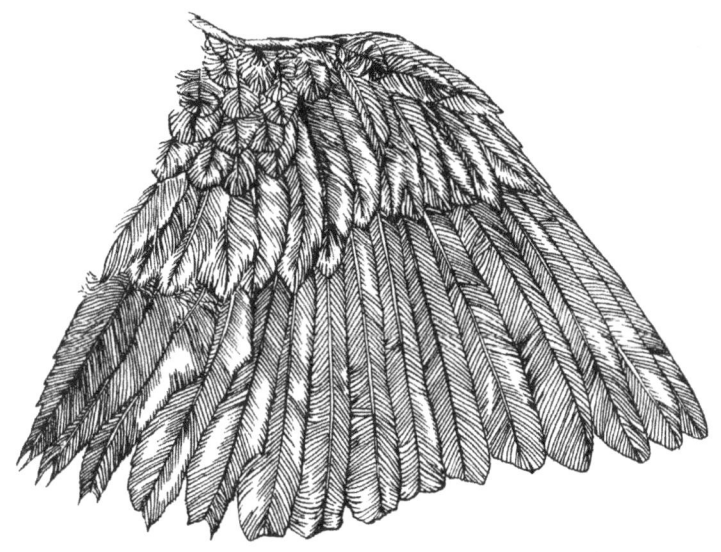

by Luke Dixon

Northern Bee Books

A TIME THERE WAS
a story of rock art, bees and Bushmen

ISBN 978-1-908904-80-5

Published by Northern Bee Books, 2015
Scout Bottom Farm
Mytholmroyd
Hebden Bridge
HX7 5JS (UK)

Design and artwork
D&P Design and Print
Worcestershire

Printed by Lightning Source, UK

A
TIME THERE
WAS

a story of rock art, bees and Bushmen

A time there was - as one may guess

And as, indeed, earth's testimonies tell -

Before the birth of consciousness,

When all went well.

None suffered sickness, love, or loss,

None knew regret, starved hope, or heart-burnings;

None cared whatever crash or cross

Brought wrack to things.

If something ceased, no tongue bewailed,

If something winced and waned, no heart was wrung;

If brightness dimmed, and dark prevailed,

No sense was stung.

But the disease of feeling germed,

And primal rightness took the tinct of wrong;

Ere nescience shall be reaffirmed

How long, how long?

- Thomas Hardy, Before Life and After

Through the wide air...there came the angry hum of bees, and two swarms, or the separate halves of one swarm, appeared hovering over the bush nearby. So it can always be in those parts, but all without a sense of menace. There never is, nor ever should be, if one moves and lives by the cautions and instincts and harmonies of a world in natural balance.

- Noël Mostert, Frontiers

My Grandpa shot the last three Bushmen in our district,

Small they were and ran like hares before his horse,

Doubling and weaving in their terror,

The first fell by the old house-fountain's watercourse.

He was the young one, lion-golden, turned - defiant -

To gain the others respite, breathing space.

My Grandpa shot him with the smooth bore muzzle-loader.

The lead slug tore the terror from his face.

His small sharp body wore the flowers of destruction,

He died with poisoned arrows in his hand,

Bird wild and more than leopard cunning,

Victim of a pattern changing land.

The other two were cornered by our Kaffirs

Against the stone enclosure of our kraal,

And Grandpa shot them with the muzzle-loader.

Three shots - three Bushmen - and no wasted ball.

These were the last three Bushmen in our district,

The families they hunted on the mountainside,

Taking the children and the girls to be their servants,

Leaving the old ones in the caverns where they died.

They were the last three Bushmen in our district.

Sheep stealers and the terrors of our herds.

Killing far more than jackals or the lions,

Fattening vultures and the carrion birds.

But now we journey yearly to the mountains

Climbing steep valleys to the Bushman's cave,

And where our river dribbles from its fountains

We creep into that high cathedral's nave,

To see the eland and the springbok and the hunting,

The elephants and the little men at war or love or play

In living line and glowing colours painted

Just as they were in our Grandfather's day.

- Reginald Griffiths, The Last Three Bushmen

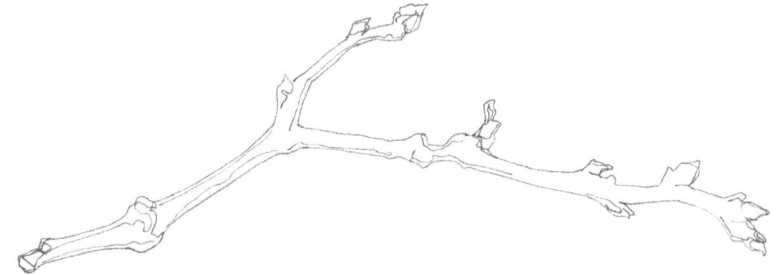

THE HIVE

This was the place.

This was the kop.

This was where the bees were.

The hive was high above him, but not so high that he could not see the bees. A thick, ever-moving cloud of them, a myriad of darting insects. Some he knew to be new bees just hatched from the crisp brittle crust that had capped the neat rows of cells in which they had developed. Free now and in the air for the first time, they were working out where their home was, tracing their movements in the sky so that when they flew off on their first journeys away from the hive they would know how to make the journey home. Like him they were trackers, like man they tracked. Other bees already knew where they were and were flying in and out of the hive, faster than he could ever run, on airborne tracks and trails that never collided.

A few bees were flying around attentively guarding the nest. These were the ones to be wary of. These were the bees that would be on the lookout as he climbed to the hive. They would dive at him once they could sense his presence and his mission. And when their diving failed to dislodge him from the rock, then they would sting, hard and sharp into him, the stings in his body ripping their bodies apart. They, he knew, would die rather than let him raid the hive.

It had been a long walk to the stony outcrop where his bees were. For they were his bees now. For the first time he was on his own, his father left behind at the camp. 'Now you are old enough, and skilled enough, that you do not need me with you,' his father had told him. 'The hive is yours to look after. You must become the keeper of the bees, harvest the honey as I have shown you, and return with it for the celebrations.'

It had been a long walk but an exciting one, the great open spaces of the Karoo to cross, with the outcrop of rock that was home to the family hive ahead of him. He relished the lone responsibility of his task and looked forward eagerly to the reception that he would get when he met up with his family and the clan that evening. The rains had come. After long, dry months the rains had come at last and tonight their coming would be celebrated. His family would come together with other families in the clan and celebrate the water from the skies. And what sort of celebration would it be without honey?

He could hear the bees as well as see them, a constant hum in the air above. Now he had found the hive he looked for the ladder that would give him the steps up to it. At waist height a piece of wood was wedged into a crevice in the surface of the rock, rammed in a lifetime ago by his grandfather. Or perhaps his grandfather's father. The first step. There were other wooden pegs above that. All were large enough for his hands to pull up on, and strong enough to support his feet as he climbed. He wasn't heavy. None of his family were, perhaps that was why they were such good honey gatherers, light and nimble on the rocks.

He had some fresh pegs with him in case they were needed to replace any that had rotted or fallen away since his last visit. The hive had belonged to his family as long as anyone could remember. As long as it had belonged to the bees. As long as stories had been told. Like his father and forefathers before him he would renew the ladder as the peg steps broke, wore or rotted away. The ladder that he climbed was the result of generations of work. Perhaps back to the time when the first beekeeper beat his drum in order that the bees should become more abundant for the people.

HOW MAN MADE THE BEES SWARM

In the beginning there was just one hive of bees. And the first beekeeper beat his drum. So much noise did he make that the bees were deafened by the sound and many of them left the hive to seek a new place to live. And so one hive became two. The following season the beekeeper beat his drum again, and again the noise disturbed the bees, and again many of the bees left the hive so that each hive again became two. So it was that in the second season there were four hives. In the third season the beekeeper repeated his trick and so the four hives became eight. And so he continued through the seasons until there were enough bees and enough honey for all of the people of the veld. Others too learned to become keepers of the bees and to cut the honey and put it away in bags and take it back home to the women.

That he knew was the story of man and bee. It happened still that a beekeeper, when bees became scarce, could bang on his drum and cause the bees to swarm and with the banging of his drum direct a moving swarm to a place where it could safely lodge and produce honey to be harvested. Now though the bees had learnt to swarm without the help of man and when the bees were swarming, it would be considered a sign that it was a powerful time to dance the medicine dance, to heal the wounds of the clan.

The bees had been making honey ever since the first beekeeper beat his drum, and man had been harvesting it, yet never taking so much that the bees struggled for food during the cold winter months. He knew that the bees made the honey for themselves but he also knew of the ancient pact between man and bee that allowed the honey to be taken in return for the gift of swarming. He had heard of some men who had been fallen to their deaths from the face of the rock as the bees had stung them. Had they been punished for violating the pact between man and bee by taking too much honey, just as the bees had once stung the head of the god Heisib, when he tried to take more than his fair share by going back to the same hive two or three times a day? Only his exposed brains had been left.

It was time to climb. The ladder snaked above him. He had made the climb many times with his father and could remember which wooden stakes to pull up on with his hands and which to push down on with his feet. And he knew the small cracks in the rock that were just big enough for a man's foot and so where there was no need for stakes. The sound of the bees above would guide him. The trick was to just think ahead one step at a time, looking no further than he could reach in case dizziness came to his head. He was wearing nothing to encumber his movements, just a small kaross from his waist that would protect his penis as he climbed.

He grabbed hold of the third stake and pulled himself up, his foot resting on the bottommost rung of the ladder. His other hand grabbed the stake above and his other foot the second stake, and so he climbed. There were perhaps sixty stakes to climb up before he would be next to the hive. He climbed slowly, on his back a bag fashioned from the stomach of a gemsbok in which to carry away the comb and honey. At his waist hung a smaller bag with his tools - a knife and some wooden stakes - and his food. He was in no rush. Time enough to look out for lichens and plants that might be worth collecting on his way. And time enough to rest and look out. After he had climbed a while he came to a small outcrop, a shelf in the rock big enough for his bottom to rest comfortably. A chubby creature with stubby legs and no tail was startled to see his face appear next to it and scampered off leaving only its droppings behind. It was a dassie, able to skip around the rocks despite its shape, disappearing into holes and crevices. He flicked the droppings away and sat down. He found a piece of dassiepis which he picked up and put in his bag. The dried and hardened urine of the dassie was a powerful medicine and it was always good to collect it when you could.

He was high now and, as he looked out across the plain, he could see a world of tracks across the landscape beneath him. Some he recognised as those of his family, connecting familiar places. Others were those of the animals that shared the plain. The elephants made the strongest, widest marks, but the antelope too had their tracks. There were the places of water, the holes that filled with the rains and could keep their water for many weeks, the streams that came and went with the seasons and the moons. Until a week before all had been dry and the water courses and watering holes just memories on the land, etched, carved into the ground between the grass, scrub and thorn bushes. Just as if his sister had drawn them on the world, her hand coming down from the sky with a giant porcupine's quill. Perhaps there was an artist in the sky who had drawn the first tracks on the earth and marked them out for the animals to follow, had made holes where the water would be and the tracks to lead to them. Perhaps that was where the tracks came from that he followed himself.

He knew the story of the Mantis and the Bee and of how the world had come into being. The Bee had been here even before the first tracks were made on the land.

THE MANTIS AND THE BEE

In the beginning was the Bee. And the Mantis.

And the Bee flew over the waters that covered all of the world. Nowhere was there any land and so the Mantis had no place to rest. Knowing the Bee to be wise, Mantis went to her and said, 'There is no place for me to stand and eat, or to lay my head for sleep.'

The wise Bee took pity on the Mantis and said, 'Come with me and we will find a solid place for you to rest.'

The Sun shone and with it came light. By the light of the Sun the Bee carried Mantis over the waters. Soon the Sun grew tired and slept and the Moon came to take her place in the sky. And so Bee and Mantis flew by the light of the Moon until she became thin and died. Through the darkness flew Bee and Mantis till Bee could fly no further. 'It is cold and dark and I am tired,' said Bee. 'I must rest Mantis.' So down she sank, and as she sank the Sun woke again and opened one eye. By the light of the Sun, Bee saw below her a great white floating flower begin to open its arms to welcome the Sun's first rays. Down flew Bee and laid Mantis in the heart of the flower. And Bee planted a seed within Mantis. And as the Sun rose from her bed and warmed the white flower Mantis awoke, and from the seed left by the Bee was born the first of the San people.

Since the rains had returned, the water courses had become wet again and the holes had begun to fill. Greenery had appeared once more as if from nowhere. He picked at a leaf and then pulled hard at the little plant till its roots came out of their tight home in the rock. The root was fleshy and moist and he enjoyed the crunch it made between his teeth and the dribble of liquor that was released.

The bees always knew when the rain was coming. They would hurry home shooting into the hive as sure and straight as his uncle's arrows or the best dart from a blow pipe. With them they would bring back nectar from the different plants they foraged on, each flower making honey of a different taste and colour: bitter honey from the little aloe, very pale, and quick to crystallise, but perfect for making kiri to drink; the aromatic fynbos honey, with a taste so delicate it was like sucking on the flowers themselves; strong tasting dark red brown acacia honey; and the strange buffalo thorn honey that foamed if you heated it.

An eagle flew high in the sky above him, swooping, skimming and diving as it rode on the currents of the air. For a while it hung above him, at one with his spirit, then it was off and away towards a smaller outcrop in the distance. That was where his sister was.

He could see her clearly, his eyes trained since he could remember on seeing the smallest things far away, like a bee returning to its hive. It was what had made him such a good honey collector. Others relied on the honey guide bird, or the night time scramblings of the ratel. He relied on his eyesight in the brightness of the days and was always on the lookout for new hives. Hives he knew did not always last forever. Sometimes a hive would simply disappear, thousands of bees gone as if in an instant, the comb hanging empty, sad and lonely in the rock. It had happened to this hive once, so he had been told, before he was born. No one knew why but one year his father had come to find the nest empty. He had retrieved all the abandoned honey and comb. It had been a big job taking many trips, but it had been worthwhile. His father cleaned the crevice of all that remained of the hive, great swathes of comb that together were heavier than he was, a gift of so much honey that it had to be shared with other families and the wider clan. And then the following year the bees returned. It was too good a place to be left without bees. Just as his clan knew the best places to make their homes, so the bees too knew where best to make theirs.

Hives were not always so high. Sometimes there were underground hives inside old termite mounds, or in the decaying root system of a tree felled by lightning. But mostly the bees kept high up, inside trees, or like here in tall cliffs and rock faces away from the claws of the ratel.

The ratel was a ruthless creature. He would destroy a hive without any consideration of the damage he caused. Sometimes the hive would not survive his raid and all would be destroyed.

THE TORTOISE AND THE RATEL

It was the Tortoise who had given the Ratel his long claws. The Tortoise was resting in the sun on a rock one day when the Ratel came by. The Tortoise pretended to be ill. It pulled back its neck until the folds made it look to be in pain. 'Please stroke my neck,' said the Tortoise to the gullible Ratel. The Ratel did as he was asked and the Tortoise pulled back his neck into his shell and trapped the Ratel's hand. As the Ratel tried to pull out his hand, the Tortoise trapped the other hand. The Ratel reached around with his foot to try to prize out his hands and then the foot was trapped too and then the other foot. The Ratel was caught by his hands and feet. With all his strength he flung the Tortoise around and tried to break the Tortoise's shell on the rocks. But nothing would release him. Eventually the Ratel became so tired that it gave up the fight and lay exhausted in the hot sun. In the heat his hands and feet decayed until they became so stunted that his claws became long and exposed with no flesh around them.

So it was that as his flesh rotted away the Ratel came to be released from the Tortoise's shell.

And so it was that the Ratel came to have the longest claws of all the animals of the veld.

And so it was that the Ratel lost his gullibility. He vowed he would never be taken advantage of again by another creature and so grew fearless, using his long claws and his heavy jaws with their great teeth to take on any adversary.

And so the reputation of the Ratel grew till all the other creatures of the veld were frightened of him. He lived by night, scavenging after dark when other animals were asleep and eating all he could find. He became the world's most fearless creature and its most feared. 'As tough as a ratel,' people said.

He knew all about the ratel. The ratel was so tough that it could eat the most poisonous of snakes and just sleep off the venom. You did not need to be a good tracker to see a ratel coming towards you, with the long white stripe running from its head down its back shining out against the blackness of the rest of its body, a streak of terror wherever it went, making a loud, fearsome *grrrrrrr…* sound when angered.

Ratels were solitary creatures, only ever seen alone unless a mother was with a new pup. A hyena five times its size was no competition in a fight. The ratel would travel great distances at night scampering across the veld having emerged from its nest in an old termite's mound, or a burrow in the ground. It liked to come out at dusk as all the bees were flying back home. Man preferred to go to the hive at the middle of the day when most of the bees were out foraging. The ratel cared nothing for the bees. It cared little for the honey. It was the grubs that it was searching for, the richest of food for a stomach that could take anything. Thousands of stinging bees would not deter it in its quest for a meal.

✾

THE HONEY GUIDE BIRD

With its black throat and pink bill, the large white patch at its ears, and yellow patches on its shoulders, and the shimmering of its wings in the sky, the male honey guide bird was designed to attract the human honey hunter. As if the startling beauty of the bird was not enough, it made a call, a soft purr to begin with and then a kind of rattling sound, like dried peas inside a gourd, or as if calling a name – *vic-torr, vic-terr*. Of course the ratel knew the sounds too and sometimes would hear them before the human honey hunters did, and the bird, grateful for any other creature which would open up the hive for him and take it apart so he could steal the juicy grubs, would let the ratel follow and not wait around for a human. But a human, the bird knew, was the better companion on a bee hunt, neat and careful in his taking of the honey, and not disturbing the bees more than necessary, so that it was easier for the bird to get in when the human had gone, take what it needed, and be away. If it was a ratel that opened up the hive there would be chaos left behind, the hive destroyed and the bees everywhere, the ratel having taken all it wanted and not caring for a moment what it left behind. There could be little left for the honey guide bird to scavenge. The ratel was also a creature of the night, no use then for the birds that needed the daylight of the sun to see by. So it was that the bird and the man were as close as the man and the bee. All three creatures, bird, man and bee, knew, and in their different ways, respected each other.

The birds were like humans in their habits, returning to the same sites year after year. The males came to the sites first and the females came after. The females, less attractive and nondescript compared to the males, having mated would move into the nests of other birds, too lazy to make nests of their own. Breaking up any eggs that she found there, the female honey guide bird would lay her own single egg in their place. The egg of the honey guide bird was not to be touched by a human, for the honey guide bird was more useful taking man to the honey than providing eggs to eat. The bird who led a human to a hive was to be left with plenty of grub rich comb as his reward. Anyone taking too much from the hive and leaving nothing for the honey guide bird would be led next time to a hidden snake or leopard.

There were other ways of finding a hive without the help of a honey guide bird. You could attach the thinnest of threads to a bee itself to make it possible to follow, or look out for the tiny black droppings that the bees left as a trail back to their hives, or listen out with your ears for the hum above. But best to let the honey guide bird do the work for you and follow the shimmering of the wings of the bird in the sun. Once found, the site of a new hive could be marked and woe betide anyone else who should come along to raid what was now the property of its finder.

THE RACE WITH THE RATEL

He had once raced a ratel, both following a honey guide bird who led them on towards the new hive. It was not an easy race to win. He had always been a good climber. But the ratel was a good climber too and could scramble up seemingly impossible surfaces. And the ratel was clever, very clever, and quite able to use a ladder left by man for his own night time hive raids. It was important never to leave the first steps too low to the ground. Make them as high as possible, just within a finger's reach of a human but beyond the reach of the claws of the ratel.

The day he raced the ratel he had heard the sound of the honey guide bird before he had seen it, like little sticks shaken inside a pot, and had known that a bird had found a hive of bees and was waiting to be followed. Perhaps it would be a new hive, one that could become his own. The bird flew swooping before him, up and down across the veld, giving him a chance to keep up. There was a ratel waiting as he ran up to the bird. The bird would have led the ratel if no human had arrived, but had waited for a better, human, companion. Usually the ratels were asleep during the day but this one must have heard the calling of the bird and come to find it, ready to scamper along in pursuit and open up the hive with no care at all, leaving little or nothing left for the bird. The bird wasn't interested in the honey but in the bees themselves, the wax, and most especially the grubs, the larvae, juicy and full of nourishment. Man would sometimes eat the grubs too, but the honey he would keep and store. It was important always to have some. And if a human honey collector knew where the hives were, the bees would store it for him as well as for themselves, to be harvested as needed. So best to take not too much and leave the bees to repair any the damage done. By the following day the wax would be repaired and the bees be carrying on as if nothing had happened.

It was late afternoon and the honey guide bird flew on ahead, shimmering in the light of the setting sun, hovering at times for the ratel and the man to catch up, then gliding ahead again. The ratel leapt along, the great streak of white down his back making him easy to follow; the man would need all his wits about him if he was to get to the honey first.

The animal's backside was in the air, a warning to those who knew that he could emit the most horrible of stenches to drive his adversaries away. It was truly a fart from another world. And if the farting was not deterrent enough his strong forelegs and claws were a match for any creature that crossed his path. Only the lion or the snake got the better of him, and sometimes not even the golden lion would win a fight with a ratel. If a lioness had to attack a ratel to protect her young cubs, and grabbed it by the neck or the back, the ratel would simply swing around, its folds of skin loose in the mouth of the lioness, and bite back. And if it was a male lion who attacked the ratel, it would swing around and bite the lion's balls. The ratel would always go for the testicles if anything male crossed its path.

Bird, ratel and man came to a tall rock with a hive high above.

He looked up at the face of the rock. He did not need the help of the honey guide bird now, though the bird needed his. He could see by the trails of wax molten into the rock exactly where the hive was. The trails of wax led upwards. When the sun became too hot even for the bees, the wax of the comb would melt and begin to ooze down the surface of the rock seeping into crevices as it slowly moved down and hardening only in the cold of the night. Then the honey would escape too. Released from its molten comb and loosened by the heat it would dribble down the rock face, out running the slower, thicker wax. The bees would be quick to retrieve it, sucking it up and returning it to the shaded depths of the hive. Bees would come from other hives, as far away as the scent would carry, and rob the honey for themselves. A thick trail of honey would soon be obscured by a cloud of bees eager to retrieve what was rightfully theirs, or steal what wasn't. That would be no time to come between the bees and their honey. In a robbing frenzy the bees would be vicious to any human who dared to interfere. But once the honey had been retrieved by the bees and every trace removed back to the home hive or the hives of the robber bees, the trails of wax would remain, darkening the rock and drawing the eye upwards.

For the ratel it had been a fruitless chase. A ratel was never going to clamber up this outcrop, however strong his claws. For him though, the honey gatherer, it would be easy. He had beaten the ratel, found a new hive and made a mark on the rock beneath it so that others who came would know it was his.

He sucked the last drop of moisture from the root. It was time to move on. The sun was rising higher in the sky and many of the bees would be out foraging for nectar and pollen from the plants that clung on in the dryness, or had sprouted with the coming of the rain.

Now with the sun high in the sky was a good time to take the honey, while so many of the bees were away, most of those who were left in the hive were too young yet to have flown, and would be working on the honey, too busy even to notice him, their heads buried in the comb cells. He swallowed the last of the root and stood on the ledge. There should have been two more stakes close by, one for his foot and another for his hand so that he could begin his ascent again. The one for his foot was there alright, just by his right knee. He tested its strength with his hand to be sure it would take his weight and hadn't become weakened or dislodged since his last visit. He was high now and could take no chances. The stake above was not to be seen and he reached to where it should have been. There was a crack in the rock and as he pushed a finger in to where the stake had been there were just a few crumbling flakes of wood remaining from the step his ancestor had left him. He took a new stake from the bag hanging at his waist and pushed it into the crack where the old one had been. It slid in too easily. He would need something thicker. The next one he chose would do the job. The rock fought against him as he tried to insert it but that was all to the good. He used all his force, his right foot pushing against the step, his other foot just touching the rock ledge with his toes, and slowly the stake moved in. When he felt it was secure he carefully pulled himself up, letting the foot step take his weight. Then with a flat stone from his bag grasped in the palm of his hand, he hammered at the new stake until he was certain it was lodged as far into the rock as could be, until he was sure he could pull himself up on to it and so continue his climb. It would take the weight of his child one day, and his child's child, just as its predecessors had taken the weight of his father and his father's father before him, back to the day when man and bee had first met.

The next few stakes were now visible above him. He watched the dassies around him, no need of ladders for them. Replacing his stone hammer he began to climb again. Progress was steady now and all the stakes were in place where they were needed. There were little outcrops of rock as well, worn smooth over the years by the feet of his beekeeping ancestors. Above him the sound of the bees grew stronger, louder with every step until they were a roar next to him. The smell of the honey also grew stronger as he got nearer to the hive, sometimes almost overwhelming in its pungency, infusing his body, making his head dizzy. He stopped again, just to take in the rich vapours, so strong that he sometimes felt he could see them as they hung around him.

The last steps brought him beside the hive itself and the comb was there next to him, built by the bees deep into the cliff face. It was clear why they had chosen to make their home here. A deep dark space, protected from the wind and the rain and from the predators who might, like him, come to take the honey. How deep it went he had no way of knowing but from the shape of the visible comb he guessed it must go in far beyond the length of his arm. He could see the edges of the wax comb. It hung down completely vertically, each comb with its outer edge towards him and the rest of it disappearing into the rock. Between each comb there was just enough space for the bees to work, those on one comb with room to move around, disappearing deep into a cell with their bottoms sticking out, without knocking into the bees working on the piece of comb next to them. It hung in nine great looped pieces, each as long as his legs. The edges were thin at the front where cells from each side of the comb came to an end, but thick where the comb was attached to the surface of the rock. The cells got fatter as they grew back from the edges, doubled on themselves, back to back with just the thinnest layer of wax between them separating one layer of honey cells from the other. Where the bees had finished their honey making, they had put a thin, white, almost translucent cap of wax on the cell, protecting the honey as food for the cold months to come. The outer combs were the newer ones, and here the honey could still be seen, uncapped, glistening in the newly made cells. It was the mature, ripe capped honey that he wanted. The bees were not working on it, their job had been done, and the honey would be thick and ripe and easier to remove.

He looked at one of the bees guarding the hive, and the bee, flying around, looked at him. There were the familiar black and orange stripes on its dark abdomen; the six legs sticking out of the body, hairy for the trapping of pollen; the brushes and rakes on its fore legs that combed the pollen into bags on the back legs; the two pairs of wings; the antennae sticking out of the head; the strange eyes that seemed to look in every direction at once; the long hairy tongue for getting deep inside the flowers it foraged on and lapping up the nectar; and the mandibles for cutting, holding and moulding wax to make the comb. And from the back of the bee, the sting that could cause such pain.

The bee saw a four legged creature, pale, with hair only on its head.

The two creatures continued to look at each other. How had this guard bee got the job, he wondered? Had the other bees chosen it? Or had it chosen itself? Perhaps the bee in turn wondered how this man had been chosen to come so close to the hive when the other humans stayed away. He did not move. If he stayed still the bee would eventually move on. Unless it decided that the man was a threat. Then it would fly into him, hitting him again and again to drive him away. Only when that failed would it use its sting. Many a human had fallen from the face of the rock not because of stings but knocked off balance by the force of the guard bees hitting them.

He watched the bees at work, their faces deep in the honey cells unaware of his presence. He loved just watching the bees. Seeing them about their work and trying to understand what it was that they did and how they organised themselves. He had learnt much from visits with his father, but there was still so much to learn. Today he had honey to collect, but in the weeks to come he would return just to observe.

As he watched the bees at work he decided which pieces of comb he would harvest. All of the comb that he could see was laden with honey. Further in the hive away from the light would be the eggs, larvae and the queen breeding and growing in the darkness. But the outer areas of comb hit by the ripening sunlight were the ones where the honey was made and stored.

If he could cut the best part of the middle combs, the bees would build down to replace them, while still having plenty more of their honey left in the outer combs. And it was on the outer combs that the bees were mostly working. On the inner combs just a few bees were checking on things, sealing the last cells, repairing bits of damage caused by the honey guide birds on lonely attempts to catch grubs, but the grubs were on the comb deep inside the hive, far away from the sunlight. It would only be when he cut into the comb that there would be much for the honey guide birds to feed on. It was not long before a honey guide bird joined him. He could feel the beat of its wings behind him as it waited for him to finish his work. Except for the sound of its wings, the bird was silent, waiting patiently for its turn. Then it would stick its pink bill into the places where he had cut across the combs of honey and reach the grubs beyond.

Best to be quick and decisive. His father had been able to cut and bag up the comb before the bees had known he was there. Today, on his own for the first time with no-one to guide him or whisper instruction, he would try to be as good a honey collector as his father had been. He had to let the stakes at his feet take his weight and his balance. Leaning his left shoulder back against the rock he could still reach to the comb in front of him. It stretched up above his head. He took out a knife from the bag at his waist and brought around the bigger bag that was slung across his back. With one hand, his left one, the one his sister used for her work, he held the bag under the first piece of comb that he planned to cut. With his right hand, his shoulder and buttock pressed against the wall, he took his knife and with a single clean cut he sliced through the comb a length from wrist to elbow. It dropped slowly and heavily into the bag. So heavy was the comb when it fell into his bag that he thought he might lose his balance for a moment. Bees flew off it and back into the hive, others continued to work away on the honey as if nothing had happened. More guard bees had noticed him and flew around his head ready to defend the hive. He took a slice of the next comb and that too dropped into the bag. He struggled with the weight, but he needed as much as he could carry and so, repositioning himself, he sliced at a third piece of comb. As it fell a flurry of bees were dislodged and became angry. One last slice and he would be done. The final piece of comb sank into the bag. It was all breaking up under its own weight. There was honey of every shade of orange, yellow, and brown, some so dark that it was almost black, some so pale as to have almost no colour at all. As the comb broke and sank to the bottom of his bag the colours gently bended into one special colour, like that of the setting sun.

The long honey bag was strong enough to take the weight of the harvest, changing its shape as the comb and honey settled within it. There were bees amongst the wax and honey, some drowning, some escaping, and others working on the comb as if unaware of what was going on. One of the guard bees did know what was happening and began repeatedly flying into him as he slung it across his back and began making a rapid descent. He knew all the steps to be secure in place beneath him and found them easily with his toes.

A few bees had stung him on his hands and arms, one or two now on his legs as he descended. But none had attacked his face, the worst place to be stung. He had seen eyes close up with reaction to the venom. Once he had been stung in the ear and that had been unpleasant enough, the sound of the struggling bee more frightening than the sting itself.

The sounds of the hive diminished as he moved down but the smell of the honey came with him. The bees above him were busy repairing the damage he had done. The honey guide bird was busy pulling out grubs in its beak.

The bag was heavy. He could carry it, and had been careful not to take more than he was able to carry. That was the way things were. If you couldn't carry it, you shouldn't be taking it.

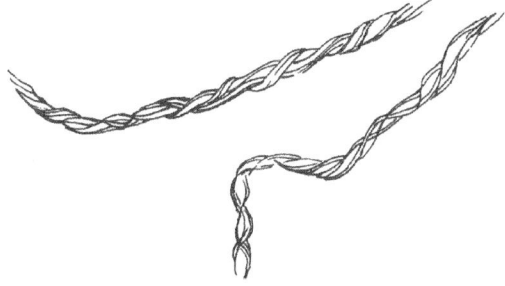

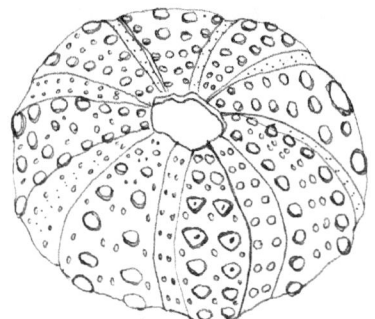

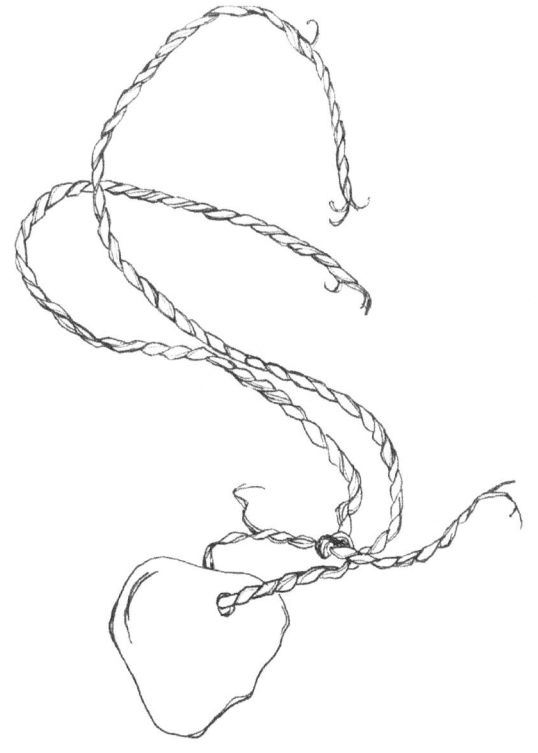

THE GATHERING PLACE

This was the place.

This was the koppie.

This was where the paintings were.

She had enjoyed the walk to the outcrop. Her bag slung across her back was not heavy and the day was only just beginning when she set off. The night world of owls and pangolins, of bats and ratels, of the civet, the aardvark and the lynx, and the little seen leopard, had retired to sleep as the sun had risen and it was the creatures of the day who were emerging, the humans, the buck, and the pesky baboons who would sit and watch people and then imitate their behaviour, singing like women.

THE AARDVARK AND THE LYNX

The Aardvark had once raised a baby springbok. When the buck was old enough for marriage, the Lynx came and stole her from the mother Aardvark. When the Lynx and the Aardvark next met, they cursed each other and have lived their lives in the darkness of night ever since.

It had been cold when she had set off and she had worn a large kaross across her shoulders as she left the kraal. Creatures were drinking the early morning dew, licking it up before the sun sucked it away. She had taken some on her tongue herself, from underneath the great fingers of an aloe, an aloe that stood almost as tall as she did.

The ground had been cool under her feet, and she had enjoyed the different textures as she walked. There was a spring in the grass on the veld that made her walking easy. Then as the ground became rockier she could feel the stones under her feet quickly becoming warm from the sun. She stopped and took off the big kaross and rolled it into her bag. Now with just small pieces of buck skin hanging in front and behind from her waist, she could feel the sun on her body. Soon it would be so hot that walking on the stones would be uncomfortable and she would need to move quickly on her toes. But for now the touch of the smooth stone on the soles of her feet was a pleasant one, a touch broken by patches of moist, soft lichen and tougher fynbos in little patches rooted into the tiniest cracks in the rock. The rocks became steeper and she started to climb. It was a gentle climb up a path well worn over many an age. The stone necklace that she wore around her neck, a present from her brother on her coming of age, played gently on her chest as she walked. Her forebears had been coming here for as far back as memory or stories could tell. It was a place to return to however far away from each other the families had made their camps. A place of coming together for all the clan. Tonight would be one of those occasions. She was sent before to make things ready. Others would come later bringing fire and food and music. But she had a task that had to be completed before anyone else arrived, a task that would take her all day and use all of the light the sun could give her.

As the sun rose, so there was sound as well as movement around her. Birds sang to one another and to themselves. The crickets called loudly as they scrapped their wings, insects not easy to see in the bushes and grass around even though they were drawing so much attention to themselves with their noise. Perhaps they were singing too and it was music that they were making. One would start and then the next, the sounds mingling and building one on another, till they were all around her, and all around each other. Were they making music together just as her clan would be tonight? Did they do it just for the fun of listening out for each other, deciding when to come in and when to come out? Or did they do it just for themselves? Because they could? To show off? Those with the biggest, strongest, noisiest wings letting the others know they were there? It was the sound of their strength and the magic powers in those wings.

Suddenly there was silence. The crickets stopped singing. The birds as well stopped singing. The breeze itself made no noise in the bushes. For a moment the world seemed to hold its breath. She too held hers, stopped and turned.

Perhaps it was the heat. Perhaps a lion. Or a leopard. Lions and leopards were to be feared. The leopard did not eat a man, but would only take a bite of him. But a lion, a lion could devour a man so that nothing was left of him. The lion's mouth was big! And the lion was hairy, with its great mane at its neck. The lions lived like man did in groups, five or six in a pride, man perhaps twice that number. Both lived within walking distance of the water, but neither would piss or shit near it. The lions drank by night, the men drank by day. A kierie could fight off a leopard and perhaps even a lion if it wasn't hungry.

She watched and waited until a gust of wind moved the air and made a sound in the leaves. A lone cricket began its song again and was soon joined by others. Far off, birds called to each other. Animals made their sounds all around her. The world and she breathed again.

THE TORTOISE

Of all the animals of the Karoo it was the tortoise that was her favourite. The small light coloured ones could move with surprising speed, and the giant leopard tortoise was big enough to have taken her weight when she was a child and given her the slowest of rides across the ground. It was said that the giant tortoise, so rarely seen and able to burrow deep into the ground for moist shelter, was the oldest creature in the world, older even than the elephant, and that it had been around as long as time itself. No-one had seen a giant tortoise with its eggs. No-one knew for sure that a giant tortoise laid eggs as the little tortoise did, or that it even had children. Maybe it lived so long that it had no need of children. Perhaps the giant tortoise was there at the beginning of the world and would be there still when the world came to its end. Who could tell? No human would ever kill it and no other animal either. An eagle could not lift it high into the sky and drop it through the air to smash open its shell and release the meat within. That could only be done with the little tortoise.

Once, a small tortoise had landed close to her, dropped from the sky by a hungry eagle. She still remembered the sound of its shell cracking open. Few things had given her so great a shock. The tortoise was a useful creature, the little one. Easy to catch and easy to cook, roasted in its shell over an open fire or in the embers of a dying one, and split apart to be eaten. The top shell was always kept in one piece. Once cleaned it was a perfect bowl. She had a small one with her today for mixing her paints, one that her uncle had given her when she was on her first painting trip. She loved the patterns on it, the stars like an inverse night sky, radiating outwards.

Halfway up the climb she paused, found a soft, flat, mossy stone and sat. From where she was perched, she could see all of her world, the land where her own people, the flats bushmen, lived. She could also see glimpses of the rest of known world beyond. The mountains far to the north, were where the mountain people with their scarified faces lived. Rarely were they met. The shore people were also rarely met. They lived by the edge of the endless sea where the shells came from, so thin and delicate and subtle in their colours. The grass bushmen had two wives and didn't talk nicely with their strange accent. She had met them some times. More often encountered were the riverbed people who knew the ways of the watercourses and the vleis and never left them. The swallows, the clay eater birds, too knew the ways of the rain. When they arrived it was a sign that the rains were about to disappear. As they flew away to the north it was a sign that the rains would be coming again. Away beyond the mountains they went. No-one knew where.

The mountains crossed the world in jagged lines of grey, their outlines softening as they reached the sky. In the distance the very air had a colour to it, a texture. She had heard of the white rain that came some years on the mountains, in soft flakes from the sky. Behind her, far away, where the land went down to meet it, she knew was the great water, the water that was always there, moving, moody and stretching away forever. One day she would find the colours to paint the mountains and the sea.

She smelt the air. Not the distant smells on the wind that the trackers sensed but the fragrances close to her, drifting from the flowers and leaves and soil around her. The fragrances that the bees would come to in their search for nectar, and that could lead her to pollen from which to make her colours. Her brother followed the bees from flower to hive. She followed the bees from flower to flower. She had all she needed today but one flower caught her attention. It was too beautiful and too laden with pollen to be passed by. She rose and walked over to it. Reaching up, her arm slid carefully between the spiky leaves, and caught hold of the stem. Gently she bent it towards her and the head of flowers came out from its prickly protection. With her other hand she took an ostrich shell dish from her bag and with a shake dropped the vivid red pollen into it. The powder made a bright splash in the shell in vivid contrast to the whiteness of the shell itself. Again she shook it and again more fell from the flower, a perfect bright fresh colour for her to use in her painting. The sunlight had yet to fade it, it was still a living thing, a part of the plant. Detached now, she would bind it and take her brush to it. Tonight the clan would see the brightest freshest colour they had ever seen.

It was a gentle climb to the top of the koppie, and she took her time. There were loose rocks and shale, and sometimes she had to scramble on her hands and knees, but for the most part it was easy going. As she came towards the top, the ground levelled and she stood on the vast flat surface. As if out of nowhere a flock of swifts, birds that never landed but were always in the sky, flew around her and for a moment she felt she was one of them taken into the air as they moved. Then they were gone and she felt the ground beneath her feet one more.

There was a wall of rock in front of her and a shallow cavern. There were large rocks around, the singing stones whose song would be heard that night. The sun was rising in the sky and shining directly on the cavern, its rays slowly coming around the dark walls, bathing them with light and revealing secrets. This was where the clan would gather that evening and the rains would be thanked and welcomed.

THE PAINTINGS

The wall of the shallow cave under the overhang of rock was covered in paintings. Paintings of animals and paintings of men, paintings of things that could not be seen except in paintings. She looked closely. She knew the images well, but it had been a year since she was last here. Some of the paintings had begun to fade, the reds in particular had not held their colour well. The sun had taken the brightness from them. Others had been rubbed and scuffed by the creatures of the rocks. Dassies mostly she thought but maybe a ratel trundling in the night or a secretive leopard hiding from the sun. Water had seeped and dripped across the rocks, depositing powder and crystals behind it. Her first job would be one of restoration. Some of the paintings she knew to have been made by her uncle, others by her grandfather. The oldest of the paintings went back many generations. Like her uncle and his father before him her responsibility was to repair and repaint where necessary, even to embellish, so that the paintings would look as good as new, fresh for the evening's celebrations. Then and only then, if she had time, she could make a new image of her own.

The painting of the eland was the one that impressed her most. It was painted to impress. She had been told it was the oldest of the images, painted many generations before. It was magnificent. A huge beast, the biggest of the antelopes with its two horns shooting backwards from its head, its whole body poised with all its weight on its great haunches. The outline was strong and thick, the richest red that it was possible to mix. More than the outline it was the shading that amazed her, as if the texture of the eland and the rock it was painted on were one. She had passed a herd of eland a few days before and remembered the eland bull dance that had marked her coming of age. That dance had changed her and her world as she had changed from a girl to a woman.

Her mother had told her :

We do the dance,

So that you will be well,

So that you will be beautiful,

So that you will not be thin.

We do the dance

That when there is hunger in the land, you will not be hungry

That when there is drought, you will not be thirsty,

That you will be peaceful in your adult life.

That evening there would be another dance:

So that all would go well with the land.

So that the rain will continue to fall.

THE WATER SNAKE

The water snake had protected her during her puberty, while she stayed in the kraal. The water snake was a shape-shifter; sometimes it would be a flicker of light, other times a whirlwind. It was a creature impossible to paint, but only to represent in paint as a monstrous creature, like the snakes of the land, but a thousand times their size. And the water snake could swim. Swimming was one of the creature's many powers. Sometimes it would appear as a beautiful young woman and lure men to their deaths, drowning in the river. For how could man swim, his body was not made for the water.

The water snake would always protect a virgin as she became a woman and began her menstruation: 'going to the river', her people called it. If a girl were to meet a water snake as she went on that journey, she would offer it a gift, a token, of a flower. She had done so herself when the flickering light she took to be a water snake appeared around her, taking a small flower from her hair and laying it on the ground at her feet. A gust of wind took the flower and the light flickered and was gone. She had not been allowed to go near the water while on that journey, lest the male rain should catch her and drown her and her family. So she stayed in the hut wrapped in the buckskin kaross. The male rain could be destructive coming with thunder and lightning. The female rain was nurturing, the veld would come to life from her caress.

As well as the eland there were other antelope on the walls. There were springbok and oryx. There were gemsbok with black and white magical markings on their faces. It was part of the gemsbok magic that they could go without water when all other animals died of thirst, moving and living far from watering holes, and not minding the fierce heat of the midday sun.

There was a painting of an ostrich, one she knew her uncle to have painted because she had watched as he had retouched it the previous year and had helped him mix the paints. While he had left her to work on other paintings alone, he wanted to work on the ostrich himself, repainting with the greatest of care. She wondered what humans would do without ostriches. What would she do? She had some small pieces of ostrich shell in her bags to mix her paints in and a whole egg to carry her water. The women used half egg shells for necklaces and other decorations. The men used their big feathers for disguise when out hunting, for like the ostrich, man was the only other two legged creature in the world that could not fly.

Slowly the images came to life as they were touched with the mid-morning sun. Tonight they would move in the flickering light of the fire and their stories would be told.

She had much work to do. Her first job was to repair the damage of time and weather and wildlife. Then she could make a painting of her own.

TOOLS

She unrolled her big kaross and placed it on the ground. This is where she would lay out her kit.

She opened her bag, made from the soft hide of a springbok killed at her coming of age, and took out her equipment, all in smaller bags and pouches. Her best paints were stored in small animal horns.

There were ostrich egg fragments and a tortoise shell, bowls in which to mix her paints.

Then there were her colours:

Oranges, browns, yellows, blues and reds of the compacted pollens her brother collected for her from the home of the bees;

The red of the soil from which everything sprang;

Powdered brown mushrooms;

Insects that would release a blood red as she crushed them;

Charcoal so black it absorbed any light that touched it;

And the black from the rock of manganese oxide;

Kaolin, the ground rock that was so white that it reflected every colour back;

And other whites, from gypsum and from lime, though the lime disappeared quickly and did not last the seasons;

Ochres from the rocks around her;

The red ochre, from the hematite that her cousins loved to use to decorate their bodies;

The yellow ochre from the limonite, the stone named after the lemons that grew on the trees to the south;

Pigments ground when the moon was full and stored in animal horns until it was needed;

Strong colours, simple colours of white and black and red, more subtle colours of oranges and browns like shades of honey;

Colours that could all be mixed to make new ones.

Then the mediums that she would use to mix her colours and make them rich, smooth, gleaming, moist and able to be fixed to the surface of the rock:

She had eland blood, most precious of all the mediums;

She had honey and wax from the bees;

Fat from the termites;

Water;

Spit from her mouth and urine from between her legs;

All as binders for her colours.

She chose a large flat stone on which to mix and bind her colours and laid it next to her implements:

Brushes made from fur, tail hair from the springbok and the rougher hairs from the hyena;

Other brushes of reeds bound to sticks;

Feathers for texture with their softness and for the thinnest of lines with their quills;

A tooth for inscribing in the paint;

Porcupine quills for the smallest details.

The site had been chosen long before. She did not know when the first of her ancestors had come to this rocky outcrop and decided that here was where they would draw the world around and beyond, behind, above and beneath them. Now the site was where they came together as a clan when events dictated or when events were to be shaped. A successful hunt, a dispute, a death or a birth, a marriage to bring families together or take them apart, such were the rites of passage that would bring people together. Or as tonight, for the coming of the rain, other forces were at work. Her ancestors had chosen the site and others before her had chosen which rocks and walls and surfaces to paint on. Sometimes the rock already held images within it; an artist could see it as the light passed across its surface, or feel it as they ran their hand over its texture. Her body was warm in the sun as she stroked the rocks. The sun caressed her and she caressed the stone. She stroked the rock gently, feeling its shape and contours, enjoying the touch of the lichen that coloured the greys of its surface, greys that had come from years of aging. The lichen trembled as she stroked it and its red and blue fronds parted under her fingers.

Elephants and elands, men and monsters were all waiting to be released from their imprisonment beneath the surface that her fingers caressed. One day they too would dance in the firelight, like the images already released onto the surface of the rock.

She was perched high above the veld, alone with the rocks she worked on. In every direction she could see the whole world spread before her. It had been a dry, dusty, yellow landscape. It had been a long, long time since the rains had come.

Now the rain had returned and her people had come to the water courses. None of the places where the water ran were permanent. For most of the time they were just dry tracks on the ground where the water might run if it came. Some would be dry for years, others fill quickly when the rain came from the sky, its legs reaching down to the ground and filling the water tracks. They had different names according to their length, width, direction and frequency of filling.

She had heard of shamans who could capture the rain animal, control it and move it from one place to another. They could summon the rains by calling on the water snake to bring relief to the dry earth. The bees too could foretell when the rains were coming. Tonight was a time to give thanks for the return of the rain, calling to the water snake who had brought them relief.

Now it was just her there.

Tonight others would come:

Her brother bearing the honey;

The men who would drum sounds from the singing stones;

Her cousins, the musicians, whose band would play while her brother danced. For tonight was his dancing night;

Her great uncle the story-teller.

The storyteller and the artist, one with words, one with images, the two coming together tonight as the storyteller would tell the stories of her drawings. And not just hers but all the others that had been made in this place. The storytellers held tales in their memories and passed them down on evenings like this one just as the rocks held stories in the paintings.

She began to make and remake the images on the rocks

There was the pleasure of making the mark, the first dot or line, the sweep of the brush across the stone. One line leading to the next, sometimes just a few lines needed to create an image. The challenge of using the fewest lines to create what it was she wanted to show. Sometimes filling in the spaces, sometimes leaving them empty filled just by the texture of the stone itself. There was something special about the feel of the implements across the stones and rocks, drawing, pulling the brush, finding new tools to work with, new colours and pigments. Experimenting. Always looking for new ways. Always looking. Seeing the world around her and placing it on the rock. Visualising the world beyond the rock, what lay beneath and bringing it to the surface.

She became absorbed in her task, becoming one with the pictures she was painting. Some of the paintings needed only the smallest of touches: a dab of paint, a clearing of lichen. Others needed careful restoration where dripping water or climbing creatures had worn the paint away, or sometimes dislodged pieces of rock. It was not always possible to tell exactly what the original had looked like and then she had to use some imagination in reworking it.

THE ELEPHANT

Reconstructing the elephant took up most of her time. It had always been a favourite of hers since as long as she could remember, but the year had not been kind to it and much of it had weathered away. She would need all her skills. With a thick brush she drew across the surface of the stone, slowly, surely, deliberately, a long arcing mark from the front of its trunk, up and around the domed head the line went, up a little further for the small hump of the back of the neck, then down the curve of the back, up again and around the huge buttocks and then down again to trace the back leg. She stopped the brush turned it and brought it across. That was the back foot.

Now the underneath. Back she went to the trunk. A flat line where the trunk touched the ground, then up another arc, the back of the trunk, up to the mouth and down the front leg. Soon she had sketched in all four legs and the sheltering belly. Last of all came the tusks, the only sharp points in all the picture, long points against the roundness of the stone.

It was almost done. The belly needed to droop a little more and the trunk to be a little longer to balance with the back foot. It took a few careful movements to make the changes. Once they were done and the outline was complete, it just remained to clean out its inside. She picked up a stone, better suited to the task, and worked steadily. The crucial thing was not to slip and break the carefully drawn outline. It was the outline that she started slowly working in from. For a while there was a solid shape of dirt and deposits in the middle of the painting but gradually this was scraped away. As the last remnant of the discoloured surface was removed, the light, almost white, elephant shone out of the rock. The sun was higher now and it caught every marking in the stone.

The hours passed but eventually all was done and she could stand back and see the whole panorama of work around her. She was pleased with what she had done, and pleased too that her own work merged smoothly into the originals that had been made so many years before. It was time for a break and some shelter from the sun.

She turned away from the rock, took some roots from her bag, and stared at the landscape as she ate her food.

✻

THE LANDSCAPE

It was a landscape of horizontals

Greens and greys.

Lines across the world, hills beyond the plains, mountains beyond the hills.

A mist hanging in the heat.

At her feet the red earth.

The trees and bushes on the veld.

Some small, some taller.

A herd of zebra so difficult to make out.

What had brought them down from the mountains?

She looked up at the cloudless sky, a lonely sky her people called it. There was no colour she could use to paint that sky. Then she looked out at the veld stretching ahead of her and down at the mosses and grasses she had walked across to get up to her painting. She felt frustration at the limits of the colours available to her. There was no paint, no pigment, for all the many greens that coloured the landscape and made up her world. There were so many words for all those greens and so many plants and insects from which surely, somehow, the colour could be taken. Her father could extract the poison from the caterpillar but not its colour. If only she had greens to paint with.

✻

GREENS

The bleached greens of the dry season.

Green so different when the rains came. Pastel shades becoming vibrant. The fynbos twinkling into flower, a carpet of green mirroring the sky above with its flower-like stars. Specks of colour across the whole landscape.

The greens of the aloe and the prickly pear.

The greens of the lichens and mosses.

The greens of the leaves of the baobab tree.

The greens of the tsamma watermelons that started so dark and lightened through so many shades of green as the days passed until they became yellow and ready to eat.

The greens of the jelly melons so tricky to eat with their sharp spines. Some bitter and poisonous (but a source of medicine and relief of pain during childbirth) others full of sweet oily jelly delicious to eat.

The greens of the shiny cacti that held their water for a lifetime.

The green of the green snake she once so nearly trod on.

There were many snakes: sand snakes and water snakes, snakes that brought bad luck, snakes that bit and snakes that could be eaten.

Green snakes as long as she was tall, longer even. Some lived in the trees and she would see them hanging, others lived in the water and she would see them swimming.

The boomslang was another green tree snake and she had learned at a young age to tell it from the other harmless ones by its gigantic eyes. She thought that with those eyes it could see much better than she could, looking for its food, moving its head slowly from side to side, its big eyes searching for something to sink its long, curved, grooved fangs into, fangs that hung down beneath its eyes, three at each side. The boomslang was a snake to steer clear of. She had seen it open its mouth to kill and was astonished that it could open it so wide that top and bottom pointed up and down directly away from each other, wide enough to catch a bird or frog or lizard. But they kept their distance and would sit up high, glistening green in the sun, to warn any person passing by that they were there. A man, even a child, was too big for a boomslang to eat and so the snake would keep out of the way of a man, lest the man ate them. Like her the boomslang saw best what was within its reach. With its dazzling green coat, as shiny as the stars at night, the boomslang was easy to spot. Not so the puff adder, sluggish, slow moving, and the colour of the ground it dwelt on. The puff adder was all too easy to step on and had a bite that could kill before the sun had set.

The glistening green of the frogs that spoke at night. How might she get the shine of the frogs' skin in her paint? The honey and wax she used to bind her pigments were shiny, but the shine disappeared as it dried.

She had the words for green but not the colours in her palette.

The red of the different aloes with their flaring red flowers, those she could paint.

ALOES

The aloe was the gentlest of plants. It opened from the ground as if two hands were pushing through the soil in supplication to the heavens, or as if to catch the rain as it fell. The skin of the plant was soft and gentle, the spikes scarcely spikes at all, just soft teeth. Few creatures were deterred by them. It was an inviting plant that could be broken open to release the balm within. For beneath its softly firm surface was the gentlest balm in the veld, glistening and sticky, nature's most reliable healer to man's external wounds, used to anoint the body after the grazes of childhood, the wounds of battle, the cuts of accident or the burns of spitting fire. All could be eased and healed with a drop or two from inside the stems of the aloes.

All the aloes flowered in winter but the aloe ferox seemed particularly a winter flower. The flowers turned from green to red in a few weeks and become as red as the brightest sunset. As soon as she saw the green flowers she was ready for them to change colour and to take the red pollen for her painting. Laden with pollen from the tall red flowers and dripping with nectar after rain it was a beacon in the long dark months. The nectar was bitter to the taste and honey that the bees made from it was bitter too.

As the stamens emerged some bees could collect the pollen, packing it into the pollen sacs on their back legs while other bees would collect the nectar. The bees were always loyal to the plants they had chosen, pollinating as they went from one aloe to another.

The aloe was the most important of all the plants and was not to be cut unless really needed. It was a potent resource. The bees kept it alive. The sunbirds too helped in the pollination, vying with the bees for the nectar.

She slid behind a giant singing stone and took a sip of water. A gecko was fixed to the rock above her, as still as stone. How long had it been there? Hours, days, weeks, waiting for an insect to come? She picked up a songololo as it inched past. How could something with so many legs be so much slower than her with only two? The creature curled into a tight spiral in her palm. She gently let it go and it disappeared between the rocks.

Before she came, the rocks had been a different colour, greys and blues and misty whites in the ending of the night, lit by the horns of the moon. The light of the sun had brought the rocks and paintings to life as she worked. Later when the sun set behind the horizon and disappeared under the earth the fires would be lit and bring the painting to life once more.

Sometimes she wondered what the sun saw when it went under the world and one day she would draw what she thought it might see.

Maybe that was where the ever-changing water snake lived.

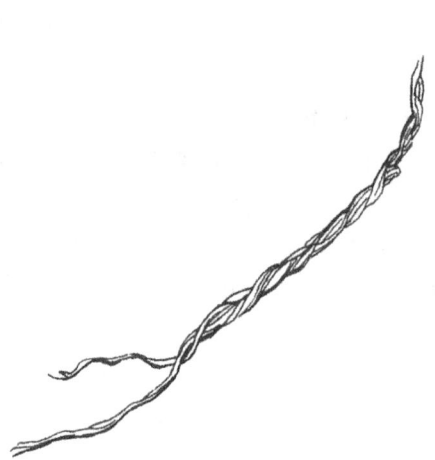

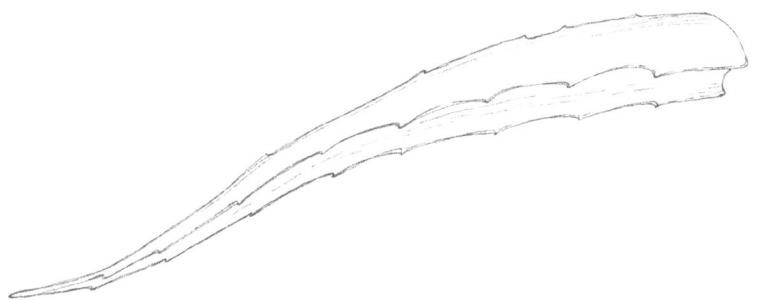

FORAGE

He was down on the ground now, the bees far above him and interested only in their hive, repairing the damage, the predator man quickly forgotten. A few bees were still in and around his bag of comb but they would soon realise that they were away from the hive and find their way home. He put the bag in the shade of a gap at the bottom of the rock he had just climbed. The bees in and around it would be drawn to the sun, and through the position of the sun find their way up and across and around and back to the hive.

While the bees sought the light, he sought some shade. The sun now was at its most fierce. All the big beasts were hidden in what shade they could find and the veld seemed deserted even to his trained eyes.

It was time to eat.

The root he had chewed and sucked on earlier had kept him going through the climb. Now he needed some meat. He always had a strip of dried meat on him, especially if the walk from home was to be a long one, or when, like today, he was off on a honey harvest. Any meat could be dried and kept for months between kills. Ostrich biltong was the tastiest. He pulled a piece from the strip in his bag and began to chew. The chewing moistened his mouth. It was a wonder that this driest of foods could awaken such moisture in the mouth. It was the sweetest biltong this ostrich, as sweet as the honey that was sinking into a sticky mass in his honey bag. Sweet but with no smell that would attract fellow scavengers, the ratels and the wasps.

His favourite food was the aardvark, perhaps because it was such a rarity. The aardvarks were creatures of the night, rarely seen even then, though heard sometimes as they scrambled into the nests of termites. In the day you could see where they had been, digging into the great red mounds where they fed on with their long, long tongues. You could see their work but not see them. They burrowed deep to get away from the sun and only ventured out when the moon could guide them.

They could be tracked of course. Anything could be tracked. And then dug out of their burrows if you could avoid their long claws. A single club on the head would kill them. They could then be baked in their thick hide, no need to skin and cut and hang first. It could, of course, be dried into biltong but aardvark meat was best eaten hot from the fire.

His parents had taught him what foods he could find for himself, veldkos, the plants and fruits and berries and roots and leaves that were all around once you knew where to look, and the bugs and caterpillars that lived on the leaves. Not all made good eating. Some would kill you, or could be used to kill others, and some could make you well when you were ill.

THE EUPHORBIAS

There were the euphorbias, the plants with sticky, milky fluid inside them. They came in all sorts of different shapes and sizes but it was the milky insides and soft prickly, spiky outsides that set them apart from all the other plants of the veld. The milky ooze could cure or it could kill. It was important to know which was which.

There was the *Gifmelkbos*, the Poison Milk Bush, with its many branches, too many to count, that grew as high as a man's chest and was covered in tiny yellow flowers.

The little *Medusa's Head* with its fat branches close to the ground and its snake like stems sometimes half buried in the ground and wider than arms could stretch, each with a handful of pink and white flowers on the end.

The euphorbia that had *Starry Spines*, sharp enough to hurt if you tried to touch the little yellow flowers but able to grow on the stoniest ground where nothing else could take root.

The *Five Eyes* with its fat stem that grew half in the ground.

The *Lion Spoor* with soft pads of green that would grow on stony ground high up in the mountains, or on rocky outcrops like this one.

The strange pointed *Many Heads* covered in branches, all getting smaller as they got closer to the top and each with a flower on its end.

The Pisgoed Bossie, the *Piss Good Bush*, was a great clump of red stems and yellow flowers as high as he was. If the ground was moist enough they would grow together in great rooted families.

The *Melon euphorbia* called so because of its melon shape, and as good as a melon to eat.

The *Caterpillar euphorbia* with its long caterpillar like shapes a source of poison.

There was much to learn about what could be eaten and what could kill. His parents and elders had taught him what to eat and what not to eat, what to conserve so it could be eaten or used another day.

THE HONEY FLOWER

The bees liked all the flowers. They would suck up nectar from whatever was in bloom. Even the tiniest yielded up something to take back to the hive. Best of all though they liked the *Great Honey Flower* sometimes called the *Touch-Me-Not Plant*. It grew higher than the tallest human. Its great leaves spread out from its stalks and if you crushed them with your hand or trod on them with your foot the smell they gave off was horrible. Worse than ostrich feathers or ratel fart. The smell was a warning to humans of how poisonous the plant could be. To humans maybe, but not to bees. For above the big grey leaves the tall stalks, as long as her forearm, had great spikes of red flowers growing at the top, so brightly coloured as to be unmissable to bird, bee or human. The flowers were so heavy with nectar that they would bend over with its weight unless the bees relieved it. Sometimes you could hardly see the flowers for the bees, or know where one flower ended and a bee began as the insect buried its head deep into the thick nectar, nectar so thick it was almost honey already. The sunbirds loved the flowers too and would come in numbers to feast. The nectar was so abundant that it dripped from the flowers into their open beaks as they flew around the plant flickering and glistening in the sun as if covered in oils and ores.

Although the plant could make you sick if eaten, it could also make you well if used on the outside of the body. The leaves could be wrapped on bruises and painful joints, or boiled with water to be used on wounds and cuts and grazes.

There was much to learn about which could be eaten and which could kill and which could cure.

Tonight there would be buck to eat. He chewed on his biltong and looked over to where his sister was working, clearly making out her figure black against the sky. He waved at her but it seemed that she did not see him.

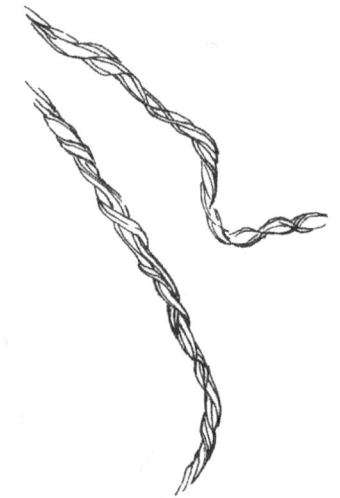

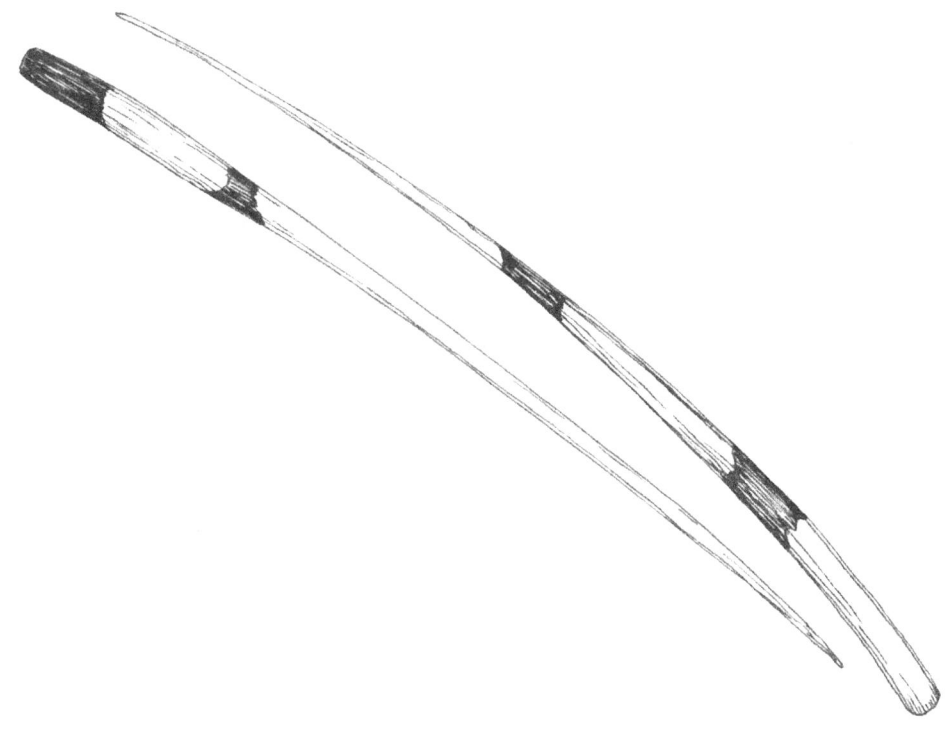

PAINTING THE BEES

She looked down across the plain to find him. Her eyes were not as good as his for seeing long distances. He could catch sight of a single insect far away, or the feathers of a bird's wing, or the cleft in a rock. Her eyes were better for the smaller, closer things, the tiny inflorescences of the lichen, the subtle indentations of the stone, the places to flake away her flint as she shaped it to make a tool.

Now it was time to make her own picture.

She held her hand loosely up to the sky and measured from sun to horizon so as to know how much time she still had before darkness would come and work would be impossible. She need not rush, she thought as she looked back at the rock.

Nowhere were there images of bees or the collectors of honey.

She would paint her brother and the bees.

She found her surface, the special piece of rock on which to make her images, tall, smooth, grey, as sheer as the one her brother would be climbing in his search for honey. It was clean of lichen but with ridges and bumps that would inspire her as she painted and which would become part of her imagery.

It was the brightest part of the day, the sun was at its highest point in the sky, its light burnishing everything that it touched. She could see every detail of the surface as she painted on it. While her brother rested and the animals below her disappeared for shade, she wanted to make the most of the light. Inside the cave and under the outcrop there were paintings that saw little of the sun and came to life only with the light of the fire. But today she was making her own special marks on the great rock outside of the cave and she would use all the advantages that the sun gave her as she worked through the heat.

She remembered when she had first tried. 'Start with a single mark, like a drop of rain,' her uncle had told her. 'Everything else will follow. It is the drops of rain which make everything possible.'

The comb first in a few looping lines.

She made marks for the ladder that led up to the comb. It gave a shape to her painting.

Then came marks to represent her brother. His arms reaching out for the honey, his strong thighs that could make him run so fast and climb so high. His head and face looking up towards the comb.

On his back she painted the honey bag that she remembered her father having, always some honey to be found with her fingers at the bottom of the bag even when everyone else thought it was empty.

And then the bees. How to draw them? She had seen them of course but had she ever really looked? And she had never been close to a hive. How many bees were there at a hive? And could she paint them all or just a representative few? Her brother had told her there were thousands, as many as the great herds of buck that had crossed the veld one year. But could she paint thousands? And they were so small. She looked at the figure of her brother and the ladder and the comb that she had painted on the rock and at the empty space around it waiting to be filled. She would fill that space not just with bees but with the patterns that they made as they flew through the sky. Handfuls of bees would be enough. She would make them as small as she could paint but more than just dots on the rock. What was essential she asked herself, to make the simplest marks yet recognisable images of these tiny complicated creatures?

There were eyes and antennae and legs and little sacs filled with coloured pollen. And there were the colours, dark browns and blacks and oranges. Best to think of the shapes she decided. The body and the wings, like crosses in the air. If she could make the shape simple enough, she could paint enough of them to fill the sky on the rock and look like they were swarming in and out of the hive and around her brother.

She used a loose piece of rock to work on first, trying different marks and shapes. Just like the portable stones with paintings on that the family took around with them on their travels. To begin with her images were too busy; too many stripes and too much detail. And they were too big. As she experimented, each bee she painted became simpler than the one before, yet still remained recognisably a bee. In the end she came up with the simplest of marks. One solid stroke of paint with an indentation either side, and from each indentation a single wing. This was the bee she would paint. She started around her brother and his honey bag. Just one at first, then another until a great cluster formed, some so close together that they almost touched. Next trails of bees heading away from the hives, others heading back. Slowly the rock around her brother filled with bees. By the time she finished, the sun had moved across the sky. She stood back to view her work. It was the first painting that was all her own. And the first painting of bees and honey collector that she knew of. She was pleased with her work, recognising her brother in the figure and happy with the way in which she had depicted the little bees flying around the great combs of honey.

Shadows were forming. The rock she was working on had cast a shadow on itself, and the outcrops and trees below had shadows too. The veld was coming to life again as the heat eased and creatures began to move once more. She sat back on her haunches and looked out. She may not have her brother's eyes for seeing the smallest thing far away, but there was still much to look at. Her eyes scanned the world in front of her.

The veld was coming to life with animals.

They had come to graze.

There were kudu far off, the biggest, craziest of the buck, able to jump a mountain it was said just for the fun of it. Good eating too for a very special occasion, when clans and families came together. A kudu could feed her family and many families besides. Its killing would be a joint effort and its meat a shared feast for many families, the cutting, cooking and drying a social effort to mark a special occasion, a wedding perhaps, or the coming of peace between warring clans.

An eland appeared. No animal was more important to the people than the eland. The painting behind her showed it in all its magnificence. The eland was the tallest of the buck, taller even than the kudu, and not as crazy. Not crazy at all but high and elegant, the greatest of the creatures sharing the plain. Too important to be killed except rarely, except on the most special of occasions.

Then she saw the springbok. One of the smallest of the buck, not as tiny as a gemsbok. The springbok had been on the earth since the Early Time, when animals were people and the people themselves were springbok.

A springbok would make a meal for this evening. The adults were as tall as her chest and the young a little shorter. Though not the height of humans they were just as heavy. They were reddish brown across their backs, like the mixed ochres of limonite and haematite, and white underneath, as white as kaolin. From shoulder to haunch ran a dark brown stripe, like the reddy-brown rust colour of dolerite caps on Karoo koppies or the brown of dried blood. The faces were white and the adults had dark patches on their foreheads. From above the eyes to the corners of the mouths ran other stripes. She had all the colours she needed to paint a springbok. Tomorrow she would return and make a painting of a springbok to replace the one that would be killed this afternoon.

It was a nursing herd of ten buck. She had heard of migrating herds, the largest herds of any of the animals of the veld, that took days to pass the settlement. She had once been told: 'The springbok are like the waters of the sea. They come in numbers to the place which is here, the springbok cover the whole place.'

They might not have been the biggest of the buck, but they were the fastest and the best jumpers, better even than the crazy kudu. They could run ten times the speed of a man and could run and jump four or five times their own height. The adult males were the best jumpers, scaring off those they didn't like or attracting the females that they did by arching their backs and jumping into the air on all four legs at the same time, leaping, 'pronking'. And the males had a funny flap across the middle of their backs which rose when they jumped and made a fan of white hairs, smelly hairs. The female springbok seemed to like it but she hated it, it was one of the most horrible smells in the world.

These male springboks were real show-offs. Springbok could go without water but as soon as the rains came, they would breed. That was when the males showed off the most.

THE COLOURING OF THE BUCK

It was the Mantis who gave the buck their colours. In the beginning there was no colour. And all of the animals were without colour. And the Mantis saw this and thought it was boring. And so he decided that he would give colour to the animals of the world and he would start with the buck, so that man would be able to distinguish one buck from another. And he did this by feeding them honey. The Gemsbok was first. This the Mantis fed with the palest liquid honey and so it was that the Gemsbok became white.

To the Hartebeest the Mantis gave the comb of young bees, and because the comb was red, the Hartebeest too became red.

To the Sable the Mantis gave the black bees themselves, and the Sable, remembering that he had eaten the bees, took on their blackness.

To the Quagga the Mantis gave the dark pollen stored in the hive and so it was that the Quagga became brown. But the Mantis did not take enough of the dark pollen to colour all of the Quagga and so it was left with just stripes of brown on its front half.

And with what dark pollen the Mantis had left, he fed the Zebra, and the Zebra too was left with dark stripes because it did not eat enough of the dark pollen to colour all of its body.

To the Eland the Mantis gave to pale brown pollen from the hive and so it was that the eland became the brown we see today.

And to the Springbok the Mantis gave the white larvae from the hive still in their cells, and so it was that the Springbok became white below and brown around like the larvae growing inside the hive.

THE HUNTING OF THE SPRINGBOK

The springbok were no longer alone. They were being hunted. She saw her close relatives and extended family getting to their positions ready for the hunt to begin.

She saw the mother bucks with their kids unaware of what was to come. The springbok had come with the coming of the rains for the springbok loved the rain. First had come the rainbow away across the sky, and then had come the rain, and with the rain the springbok seeking the fresh grass and the fynbos. It was the kids that would be hunted and one would be eaten that night. The springbok mothers looked out while their children grazed. They could see far off into the distance, further than any human, and would call out to their young if they saw or sensed any danger. The mother springboks constantly called to their young, *a a a* or *e e e*, and the young replied so that their mothers knew that they were safe. *Ma ma ma* or *me me me* they bleated in reply. And so it was that the mothers and the children kept close together and within hearing of each other.

The buck were grazing together for security, sharing the look-out, heads coming up from the grass, ears flicking in turn. There were ten of them, two hands full. Mothers and children. The buck were in front of her, the hunters beyond the buck and beyond them the sun. Her high vantage point aided her eyes, and though she could not see the hunters clearly, she could make out their presence and their positions. For the buck the sun, coming down now in the sky, would be directly in their eyes and the hunters, crouched and moving forward would be invisible.

The clan had planned for the hunt for days, as soon as they had seen the rainbow. Arrows had been fletched and sharpened. Cousins had been sent into the mountains in search of fresh wintersweet, the shoots of the plants had come up in the rain and it was easy to find them and dig up the bulbous roots full of moist sticky poison. This morning the tips of the arrows had been pushed into the roots and covered in poison. They had been carried with great care by her uncles who lead the hunt. There was also an insect that was used for making poison for arrow heads. Roasted and ground to a powder the tips of the arrows could be dipped into it. Poison had to be used with great care and some poisons were so strong that the meat of the animal they killed would become poisoned too and kill anyone who ate it.

The whole family was involved in this hunt. Tea had been made by the women from the buchu plant whose little green leaves grew on long white stalks. It was a women's plant, the tea used to ease the pain of monthly menstruation and it was the women of the clan who burnt buchu in order to smoke the hunters' arrows.

Bushes made of ostrich feathers had been prepared by the children as decoys for the hunters. She looked out again and there were the children with their ostrich feather bushes stuck in the ground. She had done this many times herself, making her own 'bush' from the great feathers of the male ostriches. She could still remember the smell of them, and knew that the children down below would smell of the ostrich as they knelt down behind their feathers. Should the wind catch their scent the buck would smell ostrich not human. It was a smell that would still be with them tonight. The springbok would do all they could to avoid the feathers.

At the other side of the herd the men had scraped out shallow ditches for themselves to hide in. Just deep enough for their bodies to lie in and not be seen by the springbok as they scanned the horizon with their great eyes. Each had marked his arrows and had them in a quiver on his back.

Below her all were now in place around the grazing herd. The women behind the children. The children with their feather bushes moving slowly forward, so slowly that their movement was barely perceptible to her, but enough to move the herd of springbok towards the men without their being startled and galloping off. Gently they moved, grazing as they went. The feathers moved in the breeze as much as they were moved by the children behind and beneath them.

There were twelve hunters, her other brothers, cousins and uncles. A line stretched out across the land. Each with a bow and arrows made from sharpened wood with ostrich feathers to guide them as they flew through the air.

It was her uncle who would take the first shot. The senior hunter, her father's youngest brother, youngest but the best of the hunters, patient and with the steadiest hand. The last part of the little finger on his right hand was cut off to make for success in hunting. It had been cut with a sharp stone, then the wound covered in juice from an aloe and bound with a reed until it had healed. He was marked as a master hunter.

They rose from the ground and moved slowly forward, so slowly that they hardly moved at all. As they came close to the herd of springbok the straight line began to curve. One of the young had become detached from the others. Perhaps it had wandered too far and could not hear its mother; she knew how dangerous that could be.

When she was small, so small that she had only just left feeding on her mother's milk, she had wandered too far from her mother and the rest of the family and been scared by the ugliest creature she had ever seen. She didn't see it at first, but heard it, splashing and wallowing in a deep puddle of mud. Then with a great shake it shook the wet mud from itself making a terrific spray across the earth and covering her in thick red brown globs. Now she saw it and what she saw terrified her. It was as tall as she was and running at her with its tail pointing high into the air. Coming out of its mouth were two great pairs of tusks pointing upwards and forwards towards her. Behind the tusks were big ugly lumps on the creature's face, and on the neck and back a thick bristly mane. She screamed and her mother came to rescue her, laughing and shooing the animal away. 'It won't eat you,' her mother said. 'It just eats grass and whatever it can dig from out of the earth.' And her mother told her the story of how, when all the animals of the world had been made, there were bits and pieces left over. So as not to waste them, out of these odds and ends the last animal was made, and because it looked a bit like a pig and had ugly lumps on its face, it was called the warthog, vlakvark, pig of the plains.

The hunt moved around the herd of springbok forming a half circle, far enough away for the animals to still be unaware of their presence. The young buck that had strayed too far was detached from the rest of the herd. For a while he continued to graze, then something caught his attention, a sight, a sound, a smell on the wind, and his neck came up, his eyes, with the black line that ran around them and across the face, stared and his ears quivered. Though he could not see them, he knew now that the hunters were watching him. The buck froze.

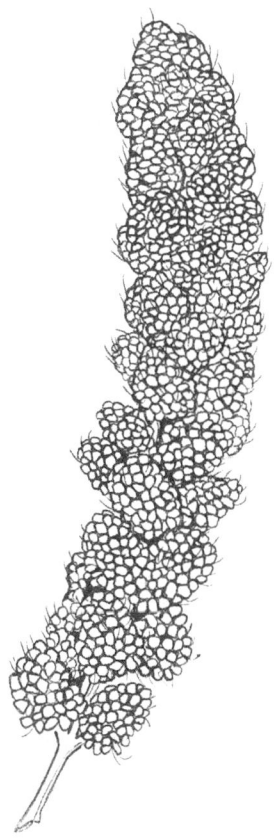

THE KILL

He looked down on the hunt.

There was stillness and silence. Nothing breathed. Not a hunter. Not a buck. Then a sound and a movement. One of the hunters pulled on his bow string and the twang broke the silence. At the same time the women threw handfuls of soil into the air. The twang of a bow to one side and a cloud of earth high in the air startled the buck. With the ostrich feather decoy on one side, they had only one way to go and it was towards the hunters. It was the wandering young kid who would be caught as all the hunters moved in for the kill. The lead hunter, the one with the shortened finger, was the only creature not moving. All the creatures of the veld were now in flight. Buck ran past him as the hunters rose, the human circle getting smaller. From above it was difficult to see what was happening. There was dust and movement and noise everywhere. But he knew from when he had been on hunts himself what was happening in the middle of all the dust thrown into the air by the hooves of the buck. One was trapped. He should not have strayed so far from his mother and the herd.

The movement stopped. The herd of buck were beyond the hunters now and feeling safe came together, alert and still. Did they know that one of their number was missing? Did the mother call out to her child?

The dust cloud came down to earth and there, surrounded by the hunters, a circle of children, ostrich feathers, men, women, was the young buck that would be eaten tonight. The young buck slowly turned and as he moved the lead hunter raised his bow waiting until the long side of the buck's flank was presented to him. The others bows raised their bows in readiness too, but it was not their job to take the first shot. Then the lead hunter fired. One arrow was all that was needed. Straight through the middle of the dark stripe along the top of the animal's belly, from shoulder to haunch. The arrow entered through the stripe on one side and out through the stripe on the other. Blood poured down from the wounds on either side, the white belly of the beast staining red as the blood ran. The men called to him, *kkou wwe kkou wwe*, so that the wounded springbok would die quickly and quietly, and be shown respect by its killers as his spirit departed. Panting, the buck trotted for a while turning to the hunter who had shot him and then began to walk towards its killer. The men kept their distance, less their shadows should fall on the dying animal. Soon its panting stopped, it became still and lay down in front of the hunters.

The dead buck would now be taken away back to the settlement. It would be cut up in front of the hut of the hunter who had shot it. A long cut down the belly and its stomach could be removed and cleaned. Blood would be drained and scooped by hand into the cleaned and empty stomach. The animal would then be cut into pieces and cooked that evening. The killer hunter would be given the meat of the shoulders as a token of thanks for his kill. What could not be cooked and eaten that evening would be dried in the sun for eating when times were hard, or for carrying on a journey as he had carried some with him today to chew on. The skin would be breied: scraped clean, worked and twisted until soft as could be. The women would make soft bags from the skin. Some would be exchanged for ochre or specularite brought down from the mountains to the north by the mountain men. He, the honey collector, would decorate himself with ochre and specularite - the wonderful rock with its dark blue flakes that looked like the night sky and would make his body glisten under the stars tonight.

They would drink honeybush tea while they worked. There was always a brew going when there was work to be done. The flowers of the honeybush smelt of honey but it was the leaves that were used to make the tea. You couldn't find the plant everywhere, and sometimes it was rooibos, red bush, tea that had to be drunk instead. But the honeybush tea was the sweeter.

❋

MEDICINES

The goodness of the bush teas were as gentle medicines. It was the buchu plants that made the best and most plentiful of remedies. He remembered having to drink an infusion of buchu leaves as a small child when overcome by the apricot sickness after gorging on too much unripe fruit.

Babies were sometimes ill with colic when feeding on their mother's breast. Then the flesh of the pumpkin could also be used for a powerful medicine, the growths on the ground being cut open and pieces mixed with cold water until the water became yellow and was ready to drink.

There was one short, thick round bush that sent its roots deep into the ground. So deep that they were not easy to dig out, burrowing down and clinging to the water below. Just chewing on a small piece of the root could make a sick person better. If a person was very sick and without the energy to chew, then the roots would have to be covered with boiling water and left until all the medicine in the root came out into the water. The cooled water would be drunk by the sick person and they would become well again.

It was the women who dug for medicines, save for the special root that men had to dig for too. This was a plant that had only short roots but grew very tall, as high as he was and beyond. Men as well as women were able to dig up this plant and pick off only the shortest, most tender of the roots to make into medicine.

Stinkleaf could be smoked, the vapours from it in an infusion that could make you sleepy when your mind was too active, and in a poultice it could relieve earache. His sister had once had an illness in her eyes and they had become red and sore. It was the legs of the great grasshopper that made her better. The grasshopper was longer than his fingers with a long black stripe down its body and wings that flashed red and yellow when it flew. It was the big back legs of the grasshopper that could mend sick eyes. They were cut off and put into the hair above the eyes and left there until the eyes had recovered. He wondered sometimes how it worked. The medicines inside the body he could understand, but how could a grasshopper's legs make a human's eyes well again?

The return walk was harder work with the weight of the honey, but he was contented with his work and his step was light. He was a honey collector in his own right now and relished the independence it gave him. The hunters and trackers always worked in pairs or teams, but honey collecting was solo work that few had the skills or courage for. He headed not for the camp but for the koppie where his sister was working and where the others would come that evening.

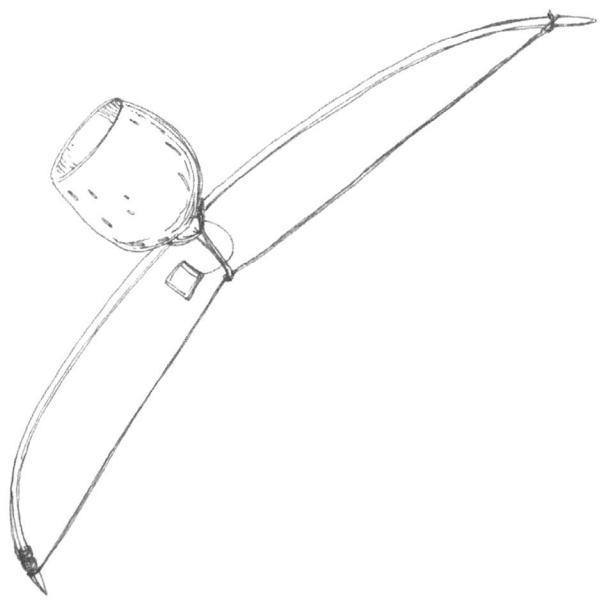

MEETING

She cleared away her painting kit, putting everything carefully back into their little bags and pouches, and waited and watched.

Eventually she saw him as he walked towards her, the great bag of honey on his back. Yes, she thought, I have captured a likeness of his body in my painting. Like him she too was pleased with her day's work and the new found independence that it gave her.

As he began the climb up to her, so much easier than the climb to the bee hive, she went down to meet him and help him with his honey. They placed it prominently on a rock where everyone would see it when they arrived and where it could be shared amongst all the clan. She showed her brother the painting. He was full of wonder and hugged his sister in joy and admiration.

She returned to her paints and brought out the specularite and a piece of fat. As he rested she greased his body with the ore and the fat so that it would later gleam and sparkle in the firelight as he danced.

The shades of the handover time cast long shadows as the sun passed custody of the earth to the moon. As the sun began to set the others arrived. Some brought the slaughtered buck. Some came with musical instruments. Some with honey wine. Long unseen relatives greeted each other. New babies were introduced. The fire was lit.

THE OSTRICH AND THE MANTIS

It was the Ostrich who first had fire. She kept it hidden under her wings for fear it should burn someone.

The Mantis wanted to steal the fire from the Ostrich. Knowing that the Ostrich had always wanted to fly like the other birds, Mantis came up to Ostrich one day and said that he had had a dream,

'I have come to tell you my dream,' said Mantis to Ostrich.

'Why should I be interested in your dream?' said Ostrich to Mantis.

'Because it was a dream about you,' Mantis replied.

Mantis told how he had dreamt that Ostrich had spread her wings in the great wind that came before dawn, and had soared in the sky like an eagle.

Next morning Mantis rose before dawn and hid in a thicket to watch for Ostrich. Sure enough, Ostrich too rose early and waited for the great wind that came before the sun rose.

As the wind began to blow, Ostrich opened her wings and the sticks of fire fell from beneath them. Mantis ran out from his hiding place, broke the sticks into hundreds of pieces and threw them in the air.

So it was that there became fire in every tree and man has been able to take it whenever he has wanted.

The foolish Ostrich never did get to soar like an eagle.

One of the boys lit the fire. He rubbed two pieces of tree together to release the fire, twirling a long, straight stick between his palms onto a flat piece of wood held to the ground by his feet. Soon there was smoke where stick met wood and the boy gently placed some bark around the smoke. He rubbed stick and wood again and from the smoke the fire sprang forth and flames danced in the bark, celebrating their release. In the morning, when the fire had died, its ashes would give life to the bulbs that grew in the soil.

Once the fire was lit, the meat of the springbok was cooked and eaten.

Dagga was smoked.

Buchu leaves were crushed to fend off the mosquitoes.

The rock gongs rang out across the veld.

STORYTELLING

Stories were told.

Stories of the early time when animals were people and when men were springbok. The stories came like the wind that blows from far away; they came through the vibrations of the thinking strings in the sky that carried the consciousness of the world, strings that snapped with the coming of death. Together brother and sister listened to the stories being told as she prepared his body for the dance, and remembered what their grandfather had once said to them before he told a story: 'First I must relax. I must sit a little till my body is at ease. Then I listen, waiting, watching for a story which I want to hear, while I sit waiting for it, that it may float in my ear.' A story could travel like the wind, told by one person from one place to another person in another place and so the stories would go around from person to person and from place to place, from family to family and from clan to clan.

KIRI

As the stories were told, the kiri was drunk. The honey drink had been prepared some weeks before with honey collected on his last trip. Mashed up and mixed with water the honey and the wax comb had been put in calabashes and clay bowls in a cool spot in the ground. The pots and gourds were covered with a hide, a small flap on the top to let out the bubbling gasses that came as the honey water turned to honey beer. The mixture would fizz and bubble for days or weeks. When the fizzing died away it was ready to drink. In the winter it was too cold for the honey water to turn into the honey drink. Without warmth there would be no fermentation.

Sometimes if the air was right the honey water would ferment quickly. Other times the process could be speeded up with broken roots from the little imula plant and a squeeze of lemon juice into the pots and calabashes. The dark honeys fermented most quickly and a drink could be made in days. The lighter honey took longer. The longer the honey water was left the more the taste would change until all the sweetness disappeared. The cover also protected the brew from predators. Powdered bark in a circle around the bowls would keep the ants at bay. They were the worst predators even though they were so tiny, and their little bodies would spoil the drink. If the root was strong enough and if the air was right, all the sweetness would be taken from the honey water, and then it would be ready to drink. The drink would taste dry and be full of potency. The drier it was the more potent its powers. The best drink was as pale and clear as the cleanest spring water dribbled it into your mouth. Just a glimpsing memory of the colour of the honey that it had come from was visible as the light passed through it.

It would be passed around in cups till all had taken a drink. Only the children would be denied a sup, though sometimes they would find a way to sneak a sip. He remembered his first drink of the honey drink when he was little and the strange feelings it had given him in his head. He'd been sick and vowed never to drink again. It was not a vow he had kept. All would glow from within with the drink as the fire warmed them from without.

🐝

THE GREAT DANCE

The storytelling ended and for a while the only sound to be heard came from the crackling and spitting of the fire as it threw its light around the rocks and the shadows of the group danced with the paintings on the walls. Then there was the sound of the bavugu, a wooden tube, being thumped on the ground. One of the older women had started the rhythm and others began to join her, until the sound of the stomping bavugus echoed around the space. So loud did it become that it echoed on the kops and koppies far away, travelling to wherever the water snake was hiding. It was time for the dancing to begin, dancing that would last until the light of dawn began to break over the distant kop where the honey was found.

They would dance the Big Dance. The women would be in the middle and the men would dance around outside of them, with their fly switches, their bodies glistening from the fat and sparkling powder rubbed onto them.

The women started to clap and sing around the fire, following the rhythm of the bavugus. Then one began to dance, sometimes turning, sometimes staying on the spot. Soon the men begin singing too, then dancing around the women first in one direction then in another. Some had dancing rattles made from the dried ears of the springbok, filled with kerri berries and tied to the feet. The songs had no words but they had names - Rain, Sun, Giraffe, Eland - sung again and again through the night with brief breaks for rest, women's clapping hands and men's stamping feet, rhythm on bavugus and drums, sustained gently while the voices were quiet.

The moon rose and hung low in the sky tonight.

It was the Mantis who had made the Moon.

THE MANTIS AND THE MOON

Troubled by the dark the Mantis took off one of his shoes and threw it in the sky so that it should become the Moon. Once a month the Moon kills a hartebeest to feed his family. From the hide of the hartebeest he makes a cloak to cover himself. Day by day the Moon's wife pulls his hide cloak from her husband until the Moon has nothing left to cover him. Then day by day he pulls it back again. When, once more, he is completely covered, the Moon hears his children cry that they are hungry and so once more he must go and kill another hartebeest.

THE NIGHT SKY

For a while moon and sun hung in the sky together but then in a flash of green, the sun was gone and the stars covered the sky. She lay on her back and watched as a handful of shooting stars traced their paths across the firmament. The Milky Way stretched across the sky. It was made when the first girl in the world had thrown a handful of wood ashes into the sky from the first fire to keep company with the stars as they make their way to bring the daybreak. There were the four great stars that marked a cross in the sky and could guide you in the depths of the night. Some stars had names to themselves: The Hare, the Winter Star, the Springbok Star. Other stars formed groups that made pictures in the sky: the constellations of the Dassie, the Aardvark and the Three Tortoises.

THE BAND

Their cousin tightened the string on his new music bow. He had been making it for weeks now, having found the perfect gourd, in shape and size and resonance, and just the right piece of wood for the stem. Oiled and decorated its sound would be heard by everyone for the first time.

The dancing stopped and the adults sat. Some on the ground by the fire, others perched up on the rocks, others tucked into corners wrapped in skins. The women did not stop but quietly kept a slow rhythm alive with their sticks on the ground.

The band began to play with and against the bavugu rhythm. Drums were tapped with fingers, a group bow was twanged by three of the younger boys, its sound resonating from the gourd in its centre, and the new bow too joined in the sound. Then one of the band stood, moved apart from the group and unwound the string on the goin-goin. As he whirled it through the air the instrument's sharp edged wooden slat swung around and made a pulsating humming sound that carried like the wind across the veld, its strange whistling notes rising above the other instruments.

Now he must dance. Those sitting by the fire moved aside and made way for him. He would lose all sense of the world around him and disappear into another, a world beyond the rocks that only dancing and his sister's art could reach. As the trance overcame him he would enter that world and take on the power and form of the substance he had brought with him that day. For honey was not just a food, for man, for the gods, and for the spirits, it was a potent power in itself.

He began to dance. His body gleamed by the light of the moon. The stars above reflected on his greased skin and became lost amongst the glistening sparks of rock that covered his body. Skin and rock and stars and sky moved as he moved. As she looked at him, his sister saw the world behind the sky, the worlds behind the rocks, and into the depths beyond. And he, possessed of the powers of the honey, powers from before the world had begun, danced and danced until the potency of the hive possessed him and he became honey.

A distant sound is heard, as if from the sky, the sound of a breaking string,

which dies away sadly. Silence follows it,

and only the sound is heard, some way away in the orchard,

of the axe falling on the trees.

- Anton Chekhov, The Cherry Orchard

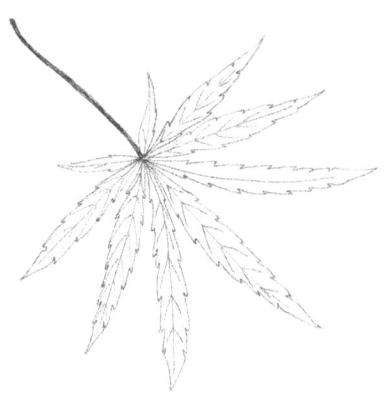

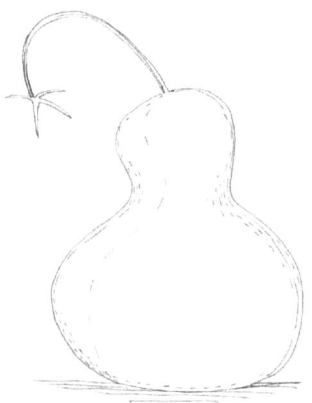

ENDNOTE

Here is no honey. I will eat honey and to procure it I shall cross the rivers Sunday, Coega and Swartkops. This country is mine. I won it in war, and I shall maintain it.

- Ndlambe, Xhosa Chief, Boxing Day, 1811

The stories of the peopling of southern Africa and of the names of those peoples are disputatious and ever changing. This is one version:

When the first Dutch settlers arrived in southern Africa in 1652, they called the indigenous people they encountered variously Hottentots (on account of their incomprehensible language and especially the characteristic clicks)   and Boschjesmans, 'Bushmen'. The first hominids had been in the region 2.5 million years before. The first behaviourally modern humans evolved from those hominids about 160,000 years ago and are now widely recognised as the first in the world. The hunter-gather Bushmen were their direct descendants.

The Bushmen are the people of this book.

Though known as Bushmen, they lived up in the mountains and down by the sea as well as in the bush. They were hunter-gatherers, taking just what they needed from the land and moving on. The Bushmen had no collective name for themselves. The people of the semi-desert Karoo, for instance, called themselves the /Xam. Others were the Ju/'oansi, the G/wi and the !Kung. (*The punctuation marks indicate vocal clicks of which there were five in their family of languages*). *They lived throughout southern Africa and north to the Kalahari; probably even further.*

There are those that say that it is from these people that all the peoples of the world are descended. Certainly they were important figures in the process of human evolution in the cradle of humankind that was southern Africa.

Two thousand years ago pastoralists came from what is now Namibia and Botswana with their Nguni cattle to graze in the lands of the Bushmen, calling themselves the Khoekhoen, the 'People People', the 'Men of Men', the 'Real People'. It was the Khoekhoen who called the people to whose land they came the San, perhaps from the Khoi word sonqua meaning 'without cattle' or simply 'inhabitants'. They pushed the San away from the coastal areas and the river areas. The two peoples became known collectively as the Khoisan. It is a word many have preferred to the often contentious word Bushmen.

About 1500 years ago, others arrived, the Bantu-speaking peoples, (Bantu being their word for 'human'), co-habiting with the nomadic Khoekoen with whom they shared a cattle-based culture. In the region of this story, the Bantu-speaking people were the amaXhosa, the Xhosa people. In Xhosa tradition their name comes from that of their ancestor, the original Xhosa chief. But others now believe it was the Khoikhoi who named these people. As they infiltrated and overran their territories, the Khoikhoi called them the Kosa, the Angry Men.

The Europeans dispossessed the pastoralists of their grazing-land and the hunter-gatherers of their territory, and made servants or slaves of members of both groups. When they arrived, the Bantu-speaking peoples too enslaved and absorbed many of the Bushmen.

The Bushmen who managed to survive lived on the margins and, after the game had been shot out, resorted to killing the farmers' stock; and so they were hunted like vermin. The last permit to shoot Bushmen was issued by the South African government in Namibia in 1936.

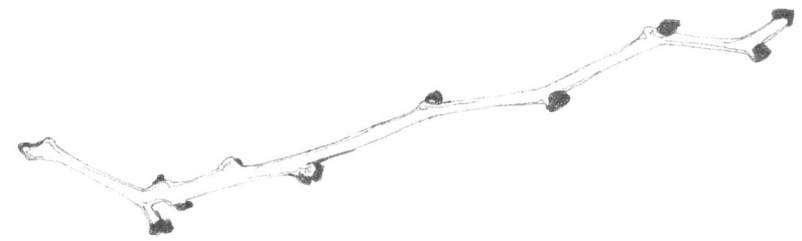

A NOTE ON LANGUAGE

The people of this book spoke no English and no Afrikaans. They did not know the Latin names for the plants they used for food and healing. Their languages were ones with sounds no European had heard uttered before they arrived in southern Africa. With very few exceptions, I have used no words from the San languages in this story but instead have chosen, where choices had to be made, English, Afrikaans and even Latin scientific names in hope of making this tale recognisable to English speaking readers everywhere in the world.

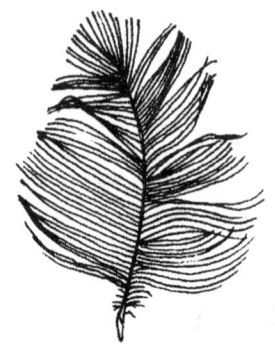

GLOSSARY

Bavugu: sounding stick.

Biltong: air-dried meat.

Brei: to work hides until pliable.

Buchu: plants of the Rutaceae family.

Dagga: the Khoekhoe name for plants of the Leonotis family, applied to Cannabis when introduced from the North by the Bantu-speaking people who themselves got it from Arab traders.

Dassie: hyrax, rock rabbit.

Dassiepis: klipsweet, solidified Dassie urine.

Fynbos: small hardy evergreen vegetation evolved in the Mediterranean climate of the Cape.

Goin-Goin: bullroarer.

Haematite: blood ore, iron oxide.

Karoo: a semi-desert region of South Africa, from the Khoekhoe word 'garo' meaning dry, hard.

Kaross: clothing made from animal skins.

Kierie: fighting stick.

Kiri: honey beer, mead.

Kirimoer: yeast.

Kop: prominent hill or peak.

Koppie: small hill or peak.

Kraal: village, settlement.

Moer-wortel: plant from which yeast comes.

Quagga: zebra like wild ass, now extinct.

Ratel: honey badger, Cape badger.

Shaman: human intermediary between the natural and supernatural worlds.

Songololo: millipede.

Specularite: iron oxide containing blue metallic flakes.

Veld: countryside, landscape, the bush.

Veldkos: veld food.

Vlei: a grass or reed lined stretch of open water.

With thanks to:

André Lemmer, who introduced me to the wonders of the Karoo and knows it better than most, for his help, advice, support and friendship;

Chris Jeffrey, who first brought me to South Africa, for his advice on names and language;

Helen Jukes, for her friendship, her conversations on bees and books, and her delightful illustrations;

Harriet Stigner, for her beekeeping companionship, and her endless enthusiasm;

Maddie Appleton, for fun-filled days out with the bees and for her trenchant comments on the text;

Andy Grewar, who took me in search of Karoo honey wine;

Paul Maylam and Gill Maylam, for historical advice, and for friendship and hospitality over many years;

Jerry Burbidge at Northern Bee Books for his unflagging support;

David Miller for his elegant and imaginative design.

Despite many efforts I have been unable to trace the heirs of Reginald Griffiths to seek permission to reprint his poem.

The Digital Bleek and Lloyd archive at the University of Cape Town has been an inspiration and is the source of the cover illustration which is reproduced with their kind permission.

The Author

Luke Dixon is a beekeeper during the summer and a performance maker during the winter.

He is the resident beekeeper at London's Natural History Museum, and director of Urban & Community Beekeeping.

His theatre work has often taken him to South Africa where he became fascinated by the old traditions of honey harvesting.

His other books include *'Keeping Bees in Towns and Cities'*, and *'Bees & Honey, myth, folklore and traditions'*.

www.urbanbeekeeping.co.uk